Worthless Wormwood and the Black Mass

A true tale of delirium and madness written out of truth

Allison Kanuit

PAGE PUBLISHING
Conneaut Lake, PA

First originally published by Page Publishing 2024

ISBN 979-8-88793-011-4 (pbk)
ISBN 979-8-88793-008-4 (digital)

Printed in the United States of America

This book is dedicated to my mom, Cathie Kanuit. She always pushes me to my limits. She said I was a rumor and a pain in the ass, but at least I got to help her realize that she was right. I was a late bloomer and a wild kid. She taught me that you can overcome disabilities no matter who you are, or where you came from. This is coming from a Schizophrenic alcoholic and dumb ass, her favorite daughter, Allison Kanuit. Thanks, Mom, for everything.

Chapter 1

*From the lips of a strange woman drop like
a honeycomb, and her mouth is smoother
than oil: but her end is bitter as Wormwood,
sharp as a two-edged sword. Her feet go
down to death; her steps take hold on hell.*

—Proverbs 5:3–23

Lucifer is the morning star and god of enlightenment. Satan is Baphomet, the half-goat beast that represents arrogance, stupidity, and the mockery of the church.

The day felt like it was tied and hung in the morning fog, pulsing, beating beads of humidity down your neck. When she awoke alone, the hardwood floor apartment seemed soaked in sweat. But still high from last night, the twisted words from last night's spell wouldn't stop playing in her mind: *from always in my eyes, from behind the skies, have wept on the morrow.* Lezah slammed her feet down on the hot dusty floor, reached down for the tray under her bed, crushed some K-pins into soft seafoam powder, blew three lines up her sore nose, and stumbled to the shining silver Deco mirror above her sturdy wooden dresser.

Suddenly, the bedroom door flew open as her frustrated boyfriend, Adam, raced in, direct and powerful, because he slept on the couch last night like every night.

Lezah quickly placed the mirror down and hopped back in bed as Adam shuffled past her. "What the hell are you doing!? Talking to yourself again?!" he croaked.

"No, babe, just can't get this song outta my head." A blatant lie as she breathed harshly with a worried face, getting up to get dressed.

"We're late! Hurry it up, you stupid bitch. Shake the bullshit and let's go!" Adam spoke sternly.

Every morning, she had to drive him to his work as a sous-chef in a small but semi-famous restaurant off Third Street in Hollywood. It was always heavy, almost stop-and-go, traffic all the way from their brick-lined place in Korea town to the restaurant.

Lezah stumbled into the living room, flopped on her brutalized Ikea tan couch, and pulled a small black glass pipe bearing a white skull from the pillows. She packed it with fat gram of some Blue Dream, lighting it with a small Bic, toasting her brain. The colors glazed round the room of the '70s concert posters and her own art hanging over the sofa of a painted-over Michelangelo's *The Creation of Adam*. Painted in silver and violet were words, "Oh thy kingdom lay in ruins."

Her mind melted. She blew out a hard full breath of pale-white milky smoke and gazed into the silver haze. Whispering into the smoke, "Of what will bring this day of secrets—mischief or drama and bullshit?" Blowing out more milky smoke, looking deeply for the answer as the smoke twisted left, whisking away into the stale sunlight, it lay stagnant through the platinum shining curtain shown squarely through the antique 1920s glass onto the offset hardwood floor.

Adam continued, yelling, "Every day, the same shit. I wake up to some shit you're screeching. Goddamn! I have so much shit to do today. I am working the middle station, and the new guy they hired can't work for shit. He's always going down in service even shucking oysters."

With his words, Lezah seemed to float over to the record player, slapping it on as the B side "Scary Monsters (and Super Creeps)" infiltrated the hot small space, cutting the bustle of the Korean market just below.

On Sundays, a Korean minister rang a small bell and preached the word all daylight hours. Not that Lezah could remember Sunday anyway. But whatever God had it in for the minister, it did not negate feelings of happiness.

Echoed shouts from Adam, "We don't have time for your shitty music."

Lezah waltzed into the bathroom, closing the bedroom door on his irrelevant negativity. She turned on the water and stuck her face into the cold, wet liquid, washing crusts of blood and chunks of blue and white powder out of her nose. Then grabbing her bottle of Ambien from the open medicine cabinet, she popped about one and a half, and soon she was feeling hypnotic like she was dancing above the world as the gentle haze creeped behind her eyelids. The world set to a majestic glow seemed to send the city to the sky. All she wanted to do was screech spells into the mirror and blaze through this world, but Adam would have nothing to do with that. At all.

It was the middle of August in Los Angeles, almost 10:00 a.m., cutting it a little too close for Adam's obsessive schedule. He had his driver's license taken away back in college. He hadn't even tried to do anything about it since they got together three years ago. With their daily trek to Hollywood and, not to mention, the nightly haul to Venice to go to their dealer's house after Adam got off at the restaurant, did not seem to faze her. She drove all of it for him as he usually was too high to drive anyway. Lezah didn't mind the drive or the pressure or his attitude because the fact that he knew nothing of her actions during the day placed her in eager anticipation of shuffling him off to work. She looked at herself in the mirror, her wild auburn hair twisted in corkscrews and tangles. The tattooed sleeve on her arm showed images of tarot cards climbing down her left arm.

She heard the speakers cut off and went to grab her keys, not willing to hear more nagging from Adam; she hurried and dove under her royal purple cotton bedcovers and dragged out her leather sandals, kicking them on as she brushed her teeth, ran to spit, then chased him to the door.

"At least the car is parked close today," Adam said while holding open the front door.

They walked out the door and headed awkwardly through the Spanish style hardwood stairs of the mission building. Lezah bobbed and stumbled on the cricking old hardwood and almost let herself giggle at the sound of the whole endeavor. The moment Adam was out of her car, her day would manifest the queerest kind of dream a person could ever be mad enough to experience.

"I would laugh so hard if you just went flying over these stairs, you old stoner," barked Adam.

"It might startle you to know I ain't one to let a couple of tumbles get in the way of me and my good time, you old angry motherfucker," Lezah spoke lightly in case he was in a shitty mood, which happened more often than not.

"At least I get up and go to work, put in my hours, and get a normal paycheck. You're just a little sugar slut making your high on candies."

They both walked out of their building at the same time into the glowing heat of this Los Angeles dead end of summer. Lezah stopped, frowned, and grabbed Adam's hips. "Is that what you think about me, babe, just some skank you picked up at culinary school?" Half joking and mind flying dizzy high, Lezah started to laugh and went to hug the six foot one blonde-haired, blue-eyed Detroit native and reminded him of why he put up with her.

He paused, gazing down at her hazel-green eyes and apologized, "I'm sorry, Lezah. I'm being an asshole, but I'm just late for the third day in a row."

"So I have to be called a sugar slut?" She squeezed him, somewhat sweaty in his arms.

He smelled like Marlboros and the cocaine they'd been doing all night.

"Just open some windows today when you make the hash caramel. I don't want you to suffocate yourself when you make all your candy," he said grinning.

Lezah had a small failing medical marijuana candy company that wouldn't have been failing except that Adam had taken 90 percent of their start-up money for *his* drugs and left Lezah with just enough to make a starter batch. Space Cadet, her marijuana candy company name, had made Lezah just under a grand of cash.

But she kept hiding forty dollars of it in a tin in her underwear drawer just in case. She had about eight bucks on her debit card but not after tonight's run to Venice. She would have to dip into the cash again merely happy that the cash was still hidden away from Adam's ready eyes. She also hid a check for $234 that was left to her after her grand-father's passing.

Lezah unlocked their green 1993 Honda Accord, the small beaten-up thing that was a punishment from her well-to-do parents for crashing her Mercedes and also for being with Adam for this long.

The car was at a boiling point, but the attraction of music in the air didn't stress Lezah in the slightest. She jumped into the driver's seat, and the Honda kicked on slowly as they pulled down Oxford Street.

Lezah closed her eyes at the stop light, turning up the volume on the radio, playing Edward Sharpe's "40 Day Dream." As she exhaled, she let her world cloud and drifted deeper into madness, hearing bizarre melo-dies play softly in the back of her mind as she drove west to the restaurant.

She was quiet on the drive. They had been talking all night, coked out, and Lezah's voice was sore and raspy. Adam was on his cell phone, managing the radio, just humming along as she pulled into the 7-Eleven for Adam's cigarettes.

"Don't worry, don't worry. I'll buy 'em today," Adam said as he pulled himself out of the car.

As she grabbed the phone cord to put her music on, she started to sing one of her own spell passages: *into the dye of the sickest wind from the ancient of the summer's dusk to the echoes of the eye of the valley laid below.* The words repeated in her ear as she closed her eyes. The world started to tremble and sparkle into a sea on a violet sky laced with grandiose ebony clouds with whispering chimes of silver tones. The air felt like the ocean as the landscape bloomed and blossomed around her. She imagined herself sitting in a deep valley of indigo grass and glittering fireflies as the chimes played slowly.

The universe rocked, and the stars seemed to escape the sky and move about in the collective waltz. *Boom!* Adam's hand slammed on the top of the car and held a water for her in the other one.

"Let's go, sweetheart!" he said sarcastically.

Lezah swallowed hard. That was close. She could have slipped too far into insanity and lose herself. She grabbed the water quickly, cracking and draining the thing in seconds. She hit the gas hard, managing to keep her music on just as the Ambien that she took kicked in, and she caught herself floating with traffic, swaying with the methodical beats by T. Rex and Marc Bolan. Stopping quickly to avoid a massive orange bus, she was beyond what you would call high and was just two blocks away from intellectual freedom. Adam smoked down another cigarette as she made a sharp turn on Orlando Street.

He pulled a vial from his chef pants pocket and pushed their apartment key down in scaly white powder.

"Better for you than an energy drink," Adam smirked as he bumped the coke into his nose.

Lezah hit the curb as she went to stop the car to let Adam out; the wheel pulled hard as the tire squeaked in place.

"Damn, babe, don't drive so harsh. You'll blow one of these cheap tires one of these days," Adam groaned.

"Bye, Adam babe. Good luck at work. Call me on your break." Lezah smiled half-heartedly, wincing with anticipation. He leaned over and kissed her before taking another bump.

"Don't do anything too stupid, babe," he said as he opened the car door. "Save your money for tonight, all right. Love ya." Adam slammed the door and started to walk across the street. Lezah smiled, she changed the way and what her lexicon would be with him. Dumbed it down, used a lot of slang so she could fit in with him and his friends. It was as if she played a character around him because he was too "adorable" with his Detroit attitude to let go. Plus he could cop drugs like no other. He once hid in a kid's trunk to get boi in Michigan. Scariest white kid you could find, and he looked like he just turned sixteen, with a blue-eyed, blonde way about him that would make you think he was too innocent to order a beer, that was till he opened his mouth.

Lezah rolled her eyes as the drugs seemed to crescendo within herself. The sun came to rest in the east as her hips sank into the car seat. She bit her lip and reached to the side door to grab a joint that she had been keeping for Adam's departure. She sparked it with her Bic covered with Mickey Mouse stickers and black crusts of ash on the bottom, a dead pothead giveaway. She exhaled this smoke smoldering around her hands, put the car in park, rolled up the windows, and blasted the awful old stereo.

"We'll dance our lifetime away at the ballrooms of Mars," Lezah sang in a misty, crooked voice. The drugs made the world magic to her. Like a never-ending trip into a mystic place full of psychosis.

She started to recall last night when she had been doing huge rails of coke on the mirror and fought with Adam about everything till dawn's early hours.

Wearing her white drugstore wifebeater and her old jeans rotting with holes, her six-foot-tall weight shifted as she swayed, captured in her dizzy sunken reality. Lezah took long drags of her joint and whispered a spell, whatever she could think of, to beckon under her breath with the beat of the music.

The shadows became heavier, and she felt it pulling her under the current of air hidden under the smog. Each movement was dragging her down as if sitting on water. The waves seemed to flow around her ankles as she drifted, seemingly sitting in a low tide now as the buzz of the city bubbled away everything itself. The radio started to drone, and Lezah opened the car door. Smoke fumed out of the car like water, and she sunk onto the ground as the asphalt turned into wet sand. She reached back to unplug her burner phone and grab her old, cracked leather wallet, then pulled herself out of the small Honda as the smokey liquid air and ashes drained out of her car. As the larger palm trees shook then began to melt into the surrounding pools of grass like feathers of green encased within the river of black cement, gravity struck the midmorning sky ablaze as a harsh light from above found her gaze through the smoke.

Chapter 2

The Voice from Above
and the Calling of Dusk

Oh, hear me in your utter cascade of grasses
wreathed in sickness and blindness.

Oh, seek not for leisure for I am but a
messenger—but not to the faithless!

Oh, hear my plight for I am an angel
of the Lord and for your will, ever
know the fate that delays your truth.

Oh, know that no sun for your path is
etched in darkness of which hollows that
will haunt and conquer pure suffering
and deepens damned's madness.

For in sorrow, you will know.

For in pain, everything will keep you.

For in nothing, time will stand at an end.

The dusk beckons and does not
come without the beckoning of
the saturation of equinox.

The dusk calls time through God's
will alone shall be done.

The dusky depth of fate's harsh reality in
tomorrow's midnight blooms something
awful that will never come undone.

Be warned.

Be aware.

Be connected.

For you are called upon by someone
greater than yourself. To walk a path
in a horror's vision collapses on this
world without mirrored hesitation.

Chapter 3

Ashes into Tomorrow's Wake

A flash of light dissipated into the sky's vile summer glow. She stared blankly in humbled shock. "Well…" she said to the emptiness of the heat.

"I will wait for God's whisper." The words came slowly as the weed smoke filled in the unstable uncertainty that pulled from today's news. Her hands shook slightly as she put out her joint on the pavement. Her mind traveled back to her youth growing up in a highly privileged family and riding six-figure horses up and down the coast at A-rated horse shows. All she wanted to do in high school was get out of her upper-class social circles and experience life in raw form. Now a gasp of true religion called and her ex-debutante-current-degenerate ass was sure as shit going to answer.

Back at the now hotbox of an apartment, Lezah threw off all her sweaty clothes and drew a hot bath. Her mind was a swamp of hypnotics, anticipation, and creeping dread.

The water dripped slowly as she lay in the bathtub. She screwed her eyes on the foam as it twisted to try to make sense of the coming days.

Chapter 4

Sickly Sullen Escapades
of Dismal Days

Mercury rising

CaspAdam-Necta-Ethos-Em

Come, silken water, awash
over my hell-bound soul.

Copper and transit light bend as
seven seas of salt compass turn
the glass light of the moon.

Open mine eye of third into
the star of the morning!

Lucifer, light bearer, fallen angel of
morning, double-cross my path and sell
the truth of passion to your word.

Nakta-Maylay-Goiyos-Reed

Spooks and sound bleed like blasphemy
on a pale horse seen with the night wild
amongst the stars. Lust in the graves of the
damned. Seek forth and find myself as I am.

Athous-Mekla-CaspAdam-Lie

With a pulse and shake of the light, it shone through the window and started to mold the tall translucent outline of an angel who had long blonde curls and a Nordic face looking like it was carved out of stone.

"Oh, my child, as my star burns bright as my pride, so grows my pity for your path, fallen at the feet of your will," he spoke soundly in a booming Bristol voice.

"Lucifer, as my shaken mind draws blank, what in the devil's mind does God have in store for me?" Lezah mused with worry.

"'Tis but a mission of offered experience in constant sorrow and vile rewards for thine shadow. Only because of your truth of heart is who you really are."

"Who am I but a schizophrenic junkie fading in sin?" she shouted.

"Oh, cursed young thing, you are but a toy to a creature who demands a sacrifice. For in the eyes of himself, blood is thicker than the water you bear, Wormwood," his tone quickened, and the light pulsed as the meaning drew near.

"If God sees my death, then I will come to a bitter end as of this moment," she whined.

Then the bath water jumped as she looked at her blue razor.

"And who said *anything* about God?" he laughed, a strong, powerful laugh as his outline disappeared and the soft light surrounding him dissipated.

She breathed heavily as tears dropped from her eyes. "Revelation! It's at of the end of the Bible." Her mind was flying as she climbed clumsily, tripping as she reached for a towel and ran to her mess of a room looking for her books. All she had been reading was

Tao Te Ching, Lao Tzu's book of The Way and the Righteous, and had committed it almost to memory. There on the floor under her bed, it hit like a thud in her heart, the black thing heavy with shimmering golden text: King James Bible.

As she picked it up, it almost felt like a million-pound weight had been strapped to her back, filled with sudden guilt of a life lived with witchcraft. Last time she began to read this thing, her eyes stuck to Exodus 22:18, "Thou shalt not suffer a witch to live." She stopped there and had not picked it up since, although the stories had been burned into her brain from growing up Catholic.

She threw it on her bed and spilled past the rose-tinted pages.

"The name of the star is Wormwood. A third of the water became wormwood, and many men died from the water because it was made bitter" (Revelation 8:11).

Chapter 5

Cryptic Script and Completely Numb

Lezah Stardust Sherman sat starkly on the haggard couch. Her biological mother had named her that when she had her at just fifteen years old and said joyously at the time "because that's what stars are made of" to a man who she was taught to be her biological father but turned out that wasn't the case. All he said back was, "David Bowie's gunna sue you."

Peter Labastson Florin was a Rockabilly base player and a Confederate Civil War reenactor who turned out to be a heartless racist and fowl lush. Lezah had snuck away from her childhood home when she was eighteen years old to meet the man after she secretly found the letters he had been sending her adopted mother who had been keeping them in her closet since she was born.

The trip up to San Francisco had been only three days long, but it had scarred her badly. It was only after contacting Wendy Andalisa Sherman, her biological mother, a year ago on the phone that she learned he was of no relation. Lezah was smitten with Wendy over the one and only conversation they shared. She was a good- hearted woman, a love-filled hippie, and a direct descendant of Civil War Union General William Tecumseh Sherman.

Tears started to come as Lezah decided to smoke herself numb. Busting out her "black death" blown glass pipe, she sucked in the smoke. In search of distraction, she put the record needle back to "Scary Monsters (and Super Creeps)" and began to pray in her own very hermetic way.

Chapter 6

Bow Our Heads in Love's Lost Time

Screaming into the midday of eve of *Lúnasa*,

First quarters of Lunar of yesterday's
nostalgic refreshing verde summertime

revelry crumbles to invoke in me peace
of mind and tempered heart with
craftsman's hand and lethal art.

Concave not into darkness
but to bind to mind

the saints of the past,

pastors of the present, and
martyrs of the future.

Echoes in mirrors vail life's secret wonder
and death's transition to ashes unknown.

Seek and you shall find rest for
the weary and ill divine.
Paint me not into the river of spirituality
that flows in a simple state of mind.

The glass coffee table began to shake with the vibration of her phone as her bitchfit of a boyfriend rang. She halfway smiled at the one person who managed to call her daily even though she had to hide her ritualistic self away when he was around.

"Hey, I only got about five till we're off break, but I got the hook on some Xans tonight if you're down," his voice low and cheaply romantic.

"Fuck yea, mother fucker! Down like a clown."

Lezah managed to coax some bravado in her words, "I got that itch, and I feel like chilling hard and passing out early."

"Well buy us some beer then, babe. What are you doing sitting on your ass? Watching Guy Fieri food porn or Anthony Bourdain?" Adam chuckled.

"Well fuck, chef, you caught me slacking. I'm up and on my way to the K-town market." She had been a line cook for some top-of-the-line Michelin-starred restaurants but quit when Adam got out of jail and made his way back into her life.

"Well, well I see. All day, every day, babe! Got to run. It's time for lunch service. Gotta make that money. Love you. See you after dinner."

She hung up the phone without a word. Beer sounded good, but the feel of today and the warning for things to come loomed over her and she sang her last prayer in the back of her mind.

Their place was on the corner of Oxford and 1st streets, right around from a large cluster-fuck of a Korean market. Adam always complained it smelled like kimchi, but she didn't mind because it was one of her favorite foods. And they had a dozen kinds.

She grabbed her keys and shuffled to the door to make the beer run.

Lezah met Adam John Harrison at the Culinary Institute of America back East in upstate New York. Back then, she was a blonde tattoo-less, ex-preppy trust fund child. She had locked eyes with him at the popular smoking gazebo in the back of their dorm, Pick/Herndon Hall.

Almost every one of her friends warned her about him, saying things like "he's not right in the head" or "he's a sleazy dope fiend who gets around." But she never listened and made him her first boyfriend she ever had. He cheated on her constantly and used her old Chevy Tahoe for dope runs. Although back then she never used heroin, she accompanied him, whipping around the backstreets of Poughkeepsie looking for dealers, almost always drunk off her ass and chain-smoking unfiltered Pall Malls.

They both had been kicked out a year into her fall session. He was suspended after his roommate called the R.A. for fighting viciously and not so secretly doing blow in his dorm room.

Lezah went back home to California and got a job at a super high-end fine dining restaurant in Hollywood. Adam moved to New York City and picked up his old job working for Chef David Chang at Momofuku.

She never heard from him until she read in the news that he got arrested for possession and stealing a cop's flashlight. She decided to write to him for her own entertainment while he was in prison.

Her dreams of becoming an accomplished chef vanished after he showed up at her doorstep. Like her mother always said, "Lezah put her life on hold for him."

Making her way down the sidewalk to HK Mart, the air was filled with the smell of tacos boiling in a vat of hot sauce. As she looked to the roach coach to her left, she remembered the one hamburger a day she sometimes lived on from that little box with wheels. But poverty and beer money skipped past the hunger in her mind as she turned the corner to get the beer.

HK Mart was shining with pale, forced white light with the loud harsh bulbs spanning the crisply organized lanes of Korean signs and pungent with hot vinegar-filled air. Lezah made her way to one of the piles of Hite beer and picked up a 30-rack. With her fingers crossed in her pockets as she stared at the cashier's perfect porcelain skin wet with miscellaneous products, she hoped wholeheartedly that her scratched blue debit card would go through.

Hustling out to the unconscious heat, she made her way out with the 30-rack resting on her shoulder. She was already swimming in sweat, sliding in her cracked leather sandals as she hauled ass up the hill to her mission temple, the apartment building of Spanish architecture painted laden forest green and eggshell white over brick. Taking the hardwood oak stairs two steps at a time, Adam could have his beer for later, all she wanted was her weed and some clairvoyants. She jammed the beer in the fridge and sat on the collapsing couch.

Chapter 7

Unholy Love and Bitter Ends

To call a casper trinity of the burning dove

Is to drive for peace, unspeakable love

How knowing truth is, willing to
drive a martyr into revelation

Calling in truth what comes incarnate

And will spill forthcoming with
force from voyages of the past

Tick like setting stones in the
sky and end this world

Full of the broken and wayside
children who turn from the sun
toward a light of heaven as they wade
deeply in the blood of the Lamb

That want only for what God is
to his kingdom as is lie in ruins
from his skull to the weapon

Bends the weed and smokes the pipe
till that which is the spirit come forth
and beckons me before my rite

"To that works well in craft, past, and art holds time well and your walk in a life to martyred in cruelty and spades," ripped a voice as loud as a whiplashed sea, "and thrice as stoned with dancing fire and worthy heart."

"Oh, burning light, will you shine a light but cast no shadow on my path as I walk with this fowl task in a quickened pace to hold to in glory through life's great fate?" She smoked her pipe with haste and a long breath.

"Oh, my madness, I will be always with you as the clouded mirror holds your eye from your truth, but tonight's future holds tragic ends," the voice touched the air in burning light.

"I hold no fear in my heart or mind as I hypnotize myself to sudden sound," Lezah whispered, drugged and bickering.

Chapter 8

Fate's Great Awakening

Night falls on the Los Angeles hideaway. The hot wood floor escalates Adam's loath and bumbling breath as he was unhappy with her lack of money, and he could not afford all the drugs that he wanted.

"Well if you didn't make candies today, then what the fuck were you up to—sitting on your ass all day?!" Adam sounded louder.

"Well maybe I was thinking about leaving you," she spoke on an impulse.

"You haven't slept in days. How could you make that choice now?" Adam shouted. "I am going to take a shower, and you think about what you're doing."

She wheeled back to her bedroom and pulled out her stash and came upon three rails of benzos and dizziness coaxed her mind.

Chapter 9

Son of Man to Nameless One

"Hello from the depths of the madness that is void of the Id and the all becoming. I call you into the depths of the course of time to lay your wasted life and take the sun from the stars and end your life," Dionysus pinched from somewhere next to the same land.

"As I sit in a dull magnificent sunset, awake in a blaze of glory filled with adventure, the dawn came upon me and spoke unto me the coming of my end. But the true light of my being, I will not die because of what I become as I am in these unbreakable bones," Lezah sounded strong, breaking the echoes in her voice.

"I am down the street, and I am coming to kill you," Dionysus cried.

A snap went a crack in her back as she hopped to the kitchen to get her Chinese Shun Chef's knife and lay in wait to the upswing of this beating drama. She grasped it in her left hand as she fell upon the couch's ottoman next to the window facing south.

She lay as she prayed in a very hermetic sort of way.

As above I lay still, do not tell a lie, and do nothing. Yet I leave nothing left undone.

With a red yarn that goes around
my body with the suits of the cards
under my left arm over the signs,

I rebuke the name of Lucifer the Liar.

Cry for sanctuary in a church that I know
down the road with King James made in
stone martyred around dark yet equal tones!

As my death, do I keep

In the steps that we keep

As I go nameless unto this venture

But hidden dark master

Behind death's great fools' player?

In a divine game, such as life,

Such as the table tips to the
weight of the word,

I lay very still doing nothing yet
leaving nothing left undone.

For which my back ties itself in knots like
the beads of a rosary and with each puzzle
becomes a lesson as I sit captured in the
ways of the righteous journey. Let it be
known that I walk in death's backward fate,
in a shadow of a name that the world knows,

Cast into prophecy of times,
massacre of reality.

I lay still and do nothing and
leave nothing left undone.

I dwell in no fear, only in belief that like the
pride stolen from my eye by Lucifer the Liar

I am a man that doesn't feel fear
but a contestant of war as I walk
through this hell that is life.

I call to bear past witness, the soul
of Ebe, to guide me not into this
fevered realm of a dark night but to
enlightenment, to a kingdom most high.

"Just call my name as I speak for the
masses as this atmosphere is harsh.
Existential manifestation is breaking
the carcass of our inherent kingdom,"
Enoch spoke out of the air clearly.
"I seek amnesty from this manifestation and
sanctuary from this motion. Can I sleep on
the floor for my morality has been called?"
"Seek the church in the dawn's light, but
speak my name and I am with you," Enoch's
voice dwelled upon the room without light.

Chapter 10

The Conquest for Freedom

The sound of a clock beat from the depths as Adam got dressed from the shower to find her baring her soul in the darkness of the living room.

"What are you doing in this darkness?!" Adam shouted.

"I am breaking up with you, Adam. I hope you don't cry for me." Lezah stood up so her current ex-boyfriend could see the knife she wielded in her left hand.

With a quick lunge, he went for the weapon, colliding with her body which drew him in like the tide. As they scuffled, Adam's raw strength powered the knife out of her hand and pitched Lezah's six-foot frame down to the floor. Feeling no pain, she hustled to the door and pushed her way to see what willed her to stand again. As new black marks appeared on her legs, she felt no fear or pain, now running down the steps into the night's truth cool tones.

A pulse ran down her back as her skin breaks the pause of the night.

"Without patience, I would be nothing, and 'tis nothing that is bound by nomenclature to be without for I am within."

Opening her eyes and not seeing anything coming to kill her, a moment of recognition rang as she wondered aloud about her own timing.

A clear voice spoke, "Forever is but a twist in a pattern of hypnosis that taps our memory." The Balthazar Razadul spoke in rhyme that saved time.

"The soul plasma plastics craft is the only thing eternal as God defines himself. I will wait for this day to bear in the rainbow of a warning sunrise. I will travel by day to the fate of my passage," Lezah spoke aloud to the air between her and the angel.

"And they all will be gods in front of that which becomes you. As you toil, it is only I who breaks your justice and brings you to the depths of psychotic bellowing and rings the back end of the book that never apologized to you," Lucifer spoke with great pride and an arrogant tone.

"To the light of the morning we break in this hot August day, I speak with the crippling gospel of the air," the Balthazar Razadul seemed to sing.

Lezah hopped up the wooden steps to her prison, called to her strategic fortitude, and braced herself to go back into the apartment. There she could lock herself in the bedroom to see a rise in the first light of a hollowed morning.

She leaned into the front door and saw that Adam was on the couch wasting away in his borrowed bereavement and counting his empty, broken half-filled cans.

Before he could speak, Lezah said, "As my parents pay for this place, I feel entitled to sleep here, but I will leave in the morning."

"Where will you go? Are you seeing some other dude and wanna go get banged out or something?" Adam asked with hate.

"You will never know where I go, but it is not because I want for sex, you shallow-minded fool," Lezah screamed as she hurtled to the bedroom and closed the door shouting, "Now leave me alone, motherfucker!"

Lezah paused in the cell of a lightless room and gathered things for her parting. She changed her flip-flops to high-cut Ugg boots and put on her white star-filled wifebeater and black yoga pants. She pushed the book of the *Tao Te Ching* deep into her boot, then took the check, put it in her grandfather's passport book that worked as her wallet, and pushed her old burner phone in the middle of the rough leather thing that held all her identification and insurance cards. Lezah paced as she waited in countered time, making herself ready, sweating as the low of the sun rose to begin what defined her experience and passage that will come with the stars. And she fell to the waves of calling herself Wormwood.

Chapter 11

Morning Rises as so Wills the World

With only two beats of old wood, the cage opened, and Wormwood snapped the door open and made her way to her hot ever-dredging tin of a Honda. She had chosen to get her check cashed from her trust that her grandfather left her before going to church.

As she turned on the radio, the songs began to change. "Oh Love" by Green Day came on, and her path seemed to make itself in stone.

Oh, fate twisted path walks

In the light of the city angels

As you call me, I am always with you

One death, hear my cry

Let the city sway

To ashes in hangman's craft

To live is to serve

Far away, far away

Waste away tonight

I'm wearing my heart on a noose

Far away, far away

Waste away tonight

Tonight, my heart's on the loose

As you brood, the weather brings to the time

Age of Aquarius

It is the darkest of the days

Oh, Balthazar Razadul and Wormwood

Fear not, only believe

And your steps will weigh themselves

For death dwells a lucid morning

Time twists from your battle

Walk with me as a friend

Forget the path of mercy

Because none will be shown to you

Call cast what you can't see

Can't kill what you create

Can't seek what to find

Ickiba-Antos-Moth-Mri-Moy

Lucifer sang when the next song
came on so twisted in possession
not to even be identified

Tempered woe and ends to enlightenment

Chapter 12

The Growing of Insanity

"I am a blind man," she screamed as her vision seemed to dissipate from the sound as the car rambled toward the bank. "As I only believe in the magic of true religion, share my fate. Oh, your fall will break the dawn in time. As I only hate to that which is the prideful sinner, this is the methos of your contempt. I rebuke you, Lucifer, and the gods that you told them they were before to that which is the Lord."

"Steady your time, Lezah, we are going to make a man out of you yet," Balthazar Razadul spoke while turning the car to pull into the bank.

Enter Gabriel

Suddenly, a queer light flickered, and a sexless woman appeared in white robe, translucent and polished.

"Gabriel!" cried Wormwood.

"You have millions of curses upon your body, and you have not had your chakras cleansed your whole life. You can barely breath, child, let me mend you and call you to attention," Gabriel spoke clearly.

"That's sounds magnificent!" Wormwood started to shake.

Chains and clogs and evil eyes came crawling out of her back as Archangel Gabriel ran her hand across the air of Wormwood's back, releasing her curses, and with a very large fat spell, a zombie slug next to her shoulder blade came out. Wormwood held her breath as Gabriel cleared her chakras that had been blocked throughout her life. The clarity of the air hit her lungs and opened her back, and it felt as though she could finally breathe. Through the light of the sun and stars, Lezah felt grounded in this tragic kingdom that were the streets of downtown Los Angeles, and her eyes began to water even though she still felt blindfolded in metaphor.

"I feel as though I can fly. Thank you, Gabriel," Wormwood said as she steadied herself to walk into the bank.

As she managed to take out the money without a stumble, she listened to Gabriel who was following her.

"Do you think my tattoos are a heretic's trash and do you find fault in me for writing them on my skin?" Wormwood asked as her arms were bare from wearing a tank top of which she almost never did.

Gabriel took hold of her arm and looked at the painted arm, colored in tarot cards, and pointed her finger at the Tower. Was it a mockery of God that scraped the sky with its blasphemy and burnt to the ground with clever David Bowie lyrics waged beneath it?

Turn and Face the Strange, after this tattoo, the wheel of fortune turned (as she pointed to her elbow) and the anti-God fell so Wormwood could reign in heaven or the eternal garden (her finger touched the top of her shoulder). The Lovers card, written in ink, sat on the back of an angel, Uriel of Revelation, mulling water in wine to tell of the coming age written in time to be golden. Gabriel looked into her eyes and said, "Your tattoo means good moral Christian values, and you should hold your head high to look people in their eyes," as they got into the car.

Wormwood started to drive, but at the gas station, sat a young man weeping, looking at a court date ticket. So she got out of the car and gave him a hundred dollar bill. He looked blankly up at her in disbelief, and she looked at the pain behind his person and felt the same.

He asked, "Are you sure?"

All she said was, "I've been there, man," and walked to the car.

Starting to the Freemasonry structure off Wilshire, shock struck her soul like lightning, and blindness cast over her eyes, with visions flashing of a robed assassin breaking into her grandfather's house, ripping the door from its hinges and walking in with silence and a motion breathing hell. As he let loose upon her father with two knives, slashing at him, leaving blood filled pieces of skin and insides—carnage that grew as he continued to force himself on all the members of her family who were gathered there. In a rage, at a boiling point of oblivion with the menace and evil that struck not an honest man, he killed all her closest family. Then like a scene in bloody history where the vision ends, the focus was turned to the beloved pugs who torn, gutted and laid in the shape of a heart with the words in blood written on the lawn of the mansion: for Satan.

Chapter 13

Bleed My Tears and Call It Truth

Strike a steel to the spine

In the blood of seven sins

To the earl of the grave

On the land in which the rot

An act of wrath to the world

In the flesh of hate

With a flash of Job

A bloodlust of a slaughter

For those who are divine

Be nothing but worthless

For you are not in the right state of mind

Two swords sewn in the raw of the blood
that beckons for the rite of the kingdom;
let fate dawn a tale that awakens the fool
who leads from behind a zealous St. Peter's
Cross in which we craft our lost mind

Belittled but believing of harsh hand
that darkness pours from our pitcher to
leave something so sweet as honey to
the devil's depth of bitter revelation

With the crimson marked with spades

As violent as a fountain filled with flesh
in blood erupted form the ethos

Written in the hand of a master of lies

For that with is sin

In the name of Satan

Where does your crying cursed eyes hold in
truth and who sits on the throne of time?

Wormwood found herself at a church as if
a light was pulling her there. Her face was

wet with tears, and her head was full of the darkness of the vision playing over to itself, wreathed in madness. She breathed in heaven and took her first steps out of the car but was struck as charmed as a cuckoo clock as the light of the Lord knocked her to the grass under a small tree beside the landmark of a lodge that was made to worship the Prince of Peace, the Lord of Lords, and the Light of Love. She fell and fainted unto the grass as her soul lay in blackness and an enclave of believers seeming to protect her against a horde of mixed hexes sounding as a cult to take her in shame and blame made themselves known.

Made in the blood with the mace of sin

The true bloodlust of a devotion to thee

The art of holding hollowed hearts

In the blood, the blood of wrath

Twisted psychological experience

With torn soul of a loveless child

With hates, cold clout of judgement that
is broken wishes for the Devil is what I
see in my own eyes, lie in wait into the
execution like a thief in revelation

Arise, the grand and adorned
Archangel Michael

And let me, the unholy, fire for my eyes,
will show no mercy on what does not
speak for *him* for that what is God

And Satan

And Satan

And Satan

Weighs upon the word and
bleeds the light to ashes

Is condemned

Is condemned

Is condemned

As I drive in hinted tinting as
the light does not beckon

for the Lord but is casted in such
blindness yet doesn't know her name

Above air

Past the star

There harkens asylum

And began to renew once more

The Ghost who is at my heels

Holds no name but preaches that what
is within the pages of days of yore

I swear and scream as I come
upon the Inferno

And my only armor was my tattooed flesh

In my blood, sick with rot, as it drips
and bleeds upon my legs held in shame

In my mind, I go insane as the blood
begins to drain, flows down my knees

I quake with the hot plague blood, crimson
menstrual blood and purple, inhered
flick and flashes of the blood that boiled
in the heat of the darkness of the car

Beats of black slips and slides
down your spine

Chapter 14

Remembering Moses

There was a black car in front of her as they drifted into a strip mall with four corners. She parked to the right, and she looked to the other side of the intersection where there was a crowd of people beginning to gather.

"Seethe to the ground, those beasts who come to violently rape and burn you witch of a tarot mess, bastardized abandonment! You're just a human being speared by an angel who escaped from the Euphrates River, and you're getting what you deserve!" screamed Lucifer.

"Lock the doors and watch yourself," Balthazar Razadul whispered in her ear.

She pushed the locks down in the Honda as a young metalhead dude came to her. When he knocked on the window, she rolled it down.

"Is there any way that I can bum a smoke?" he spoke in a matter-of-fact way. "I really like your tattoos. Look at mine." He took the ankle of his faded black jeans and showed her a bull tattoo. She looked at it with its bared teeth that was sick in symbolism of a beast that lived upon the land that was wor-shipped before the Son of God. Wormwood's tears, glistening in her hazel eyes, covered her face as the stranger walked away. She began seeing the visions of the murder and the tears ran and ran.

She sat down amid the smell of dust on the Honda. She found the *Tao Te Ching* in her Ugg boots, but with the calamity, she had lost her thirty-dollar burner phone. As she got up, a pint of black-and-red menstrual blood rushed down all over her pants leaving a basketball size red stain all over her black yoga pants. You could see the blood all over the back of her pants, seeping large drops.

"It's almost dark. Let's get in and lock that door!" Balthazar Razadul said and jumped into the car.

Wormwood locked the door to the Honda and nervously turned the car on. The sun was low in the sky, spilling a twilight haze as the light slowly drown unto the ground. Then all of sudden, there was motion all around her. She heard a shuffle of quick footsteps and the sound of a heavy metal object being placed on the top of her car. As the mechanism turned on, the world began to hum with violence as the air around her began to swim with a congruent loud howling as it shook her. She began to shake with pain as the electrocution began to drive her insane suffering. Whatever was on the top of the car was moving, the sound so heavy in a repetitive motion that it was frying her brain. She looked across the street, and out of the darkness, there was a horrible sight of a statue of a golden calf placed on the sidewalk. And in front of it, the man who bummed a cigarette was jacking his dick off while praying to the horrifying beast. Then sound struck the car over and over as a pulsing ache of hot thunder surged all through her body. She looked across the street to see a large crowd of people watching seven African tribesmen who were chanting and were dressed in the full regalia of outfits of their ancient culture. As they prayed, they held a large pole with a wooden craving of owl pointed to the now black sky.

Wormwood screamed with terrorizing pain as the machine pushed on, and the mass warred on.

On the inside of the car, there was a shadow of Balthazar Razadul sitting behind her, and the interior of the upholstery of the car manifested itself into words that looked like backward Latin. She screamed again, in anguish, as she looked to the right of the street only to see an apparition lined in blue light of the man she knew as Peter Florin, the son of Labastson, himself jacking his dick off furiously. She closed her eyes as the tears ran down her face.

She looked in the rearview mirror and saw a circle made of gold with two small gold leaves at the base. As she looked upon it, she had visions of a fowl demon with the name Nero. The cursed ritual on the blood in her pants began to leak down her knees as her eyes watered and her hair tangled; she screamed as she realized she was a sacrifice unto the unholy night.

Torture of unholy sin in the
dead of the darkness

With a flash as the light hits the sky

In the shadow of an unholy night

With an electric whistle that cuts like a bite

In the lust-filled crescendo of fright

Lit by a golden calf's ungodly sight

With the son of the Labastson's cursed soul

In a world of the days of old

Begs a martyr being muted by the profound

Of a mechanism that breaks the sound

Of the beast that dance upon the ground

As the tribesmen who rain hell upside down

In the tiny tin of a car being forced round

With the pain in the eyes of death

As they torture of a Lamb
baring nothing but shame

As the whips leach and blast the back of
a man who died once before he came

As the visions pour into crying eyes of yore

Of the deep pain that burns the magnetic
rage of punishing paradox written in
blood before it was written in black ink

As the lamb's blood clots in pain,
enough to drive a madman insane

As the villains worship a God who is
condemned by name, and the blind
man's light rallies life's tormented game

Chapter 15

Antichrist Apocalyptic

The sound droned on louder now over the taunting and chanting of the African tribesmen. One dressed in all sticks and his wood face looked familiar, he was a short Black man with a graying beard.

Gabriel spoke, "That one thinks he's Pey himself."

The sound from the machine whipped on creating an electrical pain down her spine; her vision was colorless of a bizarre language with flipped V ran past her eyes.

She screamed as more and more trauma ensued.

The tribesmen continued dancing around an owl on a long pole and screaming into the night. The young metalhead man was on his knees violently worshipping the golden bull statue to her left.

Then the night continued.

Dancing in sin

Pulse, pulse, pulse

Spin, spin, spin

Electric pain all though my skin

My bones don't know that its
heart is still bleeding

And kingdom was made in life meaning

Pulse, pulse, pulse

Spin, spin, spin

As the execution truly begins

Streaks and screams

Death and judgement

Blood and pain will not do you justice

Pulse, pulse, pulse

Spin, spin, spin

Crucifixion of the modern age
sees nobody ever to win

Look into the horrible, twisted
sidewalk as the blasphemy feeds
the beast that dance in sin

Pulse, pulse, pulse

Spin, spin, spin

You can't be just a saint to win

Chapter 16

The Confidence of Lunacy

As the horror of it all beat on, the pain of electricity beat through Wormwood's body, and she started hearing the screams of a man she knew. Gabriel said that the angels saved this man as a twelve-year-old boy when he was going to hang himself with a belt in his closet.

With the motion of the cars, the man cried out for his mother. As the spinning pain began to get louder, the cries came from the cars that drove back and forth from the intersection.

Wormwood screamed and closed her eyes and saw a vision of a man standing with a mirror image of himself in a fiery circle of a star, and she heard the voice of an angel that said, "That is eternal hell."

Then she saw a vision of one of the tribesmen with seven mirrored images of himself back to back in a fire-filled star; an angel spoke, "That would be eternal damnation."

Wormwood screamed as the pain began pounding, and the tribesmen danced on. Her hair twisted up as she cried, but every time she closed her eyes, another vision appeared mostly of a figure of a soul turning through the void with two scythes moving effortlessly through the darkness. It had been hours since

the torture began. She cried as words written
in dust appeared that read: Bred and Yesod.

Interplastic radio

Sound of broken thunder

Tears and screams in black summer night

Cast down tears away from sanity's grip

Violating violent visionary

Mythical mind melting madness

Tears and screams in bloody shame

Electric currents ripping my mind to slip

Midnight masquerade missionary

Centrical serenading sadness

Tears and screams of gold bull's blasphemy

Nameless Bartholomew's tragedy

Arise a man who's lived beside every profit
that's gone blind, to wait in a sudden
death willing to go to her last breath

To a Psalm that's not happened yet

Awakened in the night of absolute death

Bloody execution event

Death in revelation as the beasts run round

To the gallows, to the heretic,
to rope, to the flame

Death in unbreakable bones,
not a son of man

God help us all, but abandon all hope

Tears and screams knowing not your name

And the night continued

Dancing in sin

Pulse, pulse, pulse

Spin, spin, spin

Electric pain all though my skin

My bones don't know that
it's a heart still beating

And kingdom was made in life meaning

Pulse, pulse, pulse

Spin, spin, spin

As the execution truly begins

Streaks and screams

Death and judgement

Blood and pain will not do you justice

Pulse, pulse, pulse

Spin, spin, spin

Crucifixion of the modern age
sees nobody ever to win

Look into the horrible, twisted
sidewalk as the blasphemy feeds
the beast that dance in sin

Pulse, pulse, pulse

Spin, spin, spin

You can't be just a saint to win

Interplastic radio

Seek into the marrow

Cry your eyes out

Twist the sound, break the night,
hold tight to your faith

As fate pushes the magnetic sound,
a pain pushes the air around

Struck down, struck up,
electrical whip duel hits

Shock screams full hit

Sharp pain bleeds black

Turn far, faint a little

Wreath the windows' half-past lightning

Brush the Latin off your walls

Second the coming until the dawn,
know the words to the half-assed song

Break the light, and awaken the sun

For what was done was more than wrong

Chapter 17

Madness Morning on an August Morning

The sun broke the earth in two as it hit Wormwood's face, the anger in her bones began to shake. The tribesmen were still there, now pounding their shafts against the ground. Someone came up beside her car and took the device off her car. The golden bull was gone and so was the image of Peter Labastson Florin—all had whisked away. She stared in the rearview mirror, her eyes swollen crimson with wrath, then she started moving her hand across her face. Pestilence, she spelled out with one fluid motion; and again, pestilence as she lit her eyes into the eyes of the tribesmen.

With the fire, the throne, and the
charisma of the muck and the mire

With thorns of the fate and
the blood of the lamb

With the bones of the spine, I
know exactly who I am

WORTHLESS WORMWOOD AND THE BLACK MASS

In the hunt of a name and
a shadow of a ghost

Pestilence is never whom you love the most

With the blood rolling down my knee

I know this kingdom is not
only eternal to thee

As I cast my might to strike
like a thief in night

To the hallow held high

Righteous are the few who come unto thee
for the tragic state of no mercy unto you

Pestilence testament to the heathen sight

In this torture in this tournament
in my heart's blackest night

To the shallow of the graves of
the mighty who have fallen

As my hand moves my mind in
front of my eyes, bright pestilence
testament to all hell's bite

Sacrifice unto this unholy morning light

Chapter 18

The Test of Death

Wormwood's head was spinning now, her mind ablazed and acting on pure will alone. The morning was already hot with woe and hot weather, so she kicked off her Ugg boots and quested for water. Holding her hand above her eyes and her mind raped in madness and brutally hypnotized, she pictured herself just in her bones with no skin to be known. She opened the door from her electric cage car and stuck unto the ground her bare feet with only burning sandy concrete and the eyes of the mass who bear witness to this madness. She began to walk backward to a small Mexican restaurant in a strip mall and followed by a gothic shadow of a man, Balthazar Razadul.

God Among Men

The "I," the "Id," the hate, and the lordship

Deaths in death bones

Leading backward with the left heel

As the sun beats the son still bleeds

Even and odd path for water

Eyes covered and blind turning pages to Job
for thy testament deaths in death bones

I pray to John of Revelation, "I only mourn
the *holy* as this day will know its *glory*"

Death in death bones

'Tis the days were the devil gets his
due but only by the ways of you

One foot behind, the other marching,
scorching skin, *blood,* oh! *blood*
streaming down, thighs wet with it

All held tight by a masonry
mastered tattooed thing

Death in death bones

Cursed are the words we
keep from the villains

(now the victims)

As the "it" that "is" quest for water
rolls backward past it all

Twenty steps 'til Wormwood's heels hit
the curb of the strip mall's corner store. As
a cry of many angels rang into the sky, "It
was written in blood before it was written in
stone! A prophecy has been fulfilled."

Her eyes never stopped crying as she
removed her hand from her eyes; a vision
came over her of something with black condemned bones. It arose from the center of
the earth, as the Tao itself, of the void that
surrounds a neon circular rainbow. The skel-
eton itself did not move, but the earth moved
around it. As the vision began to fade, the

cult of men cried out, "It is Satan herself. *It is Satan herself!*"

Blurry was her vision as she walked into the Mexican restaurant. The owner eyed her and shook his head. Wormwood was covered in menstrual blood, her hair red with dread-locks and her eyes brimming with tears, eye-liner streaming down her face. The world spun around her from whatever machine was put on her car that twirled to whirl the world around her mind. She stood at the cash register and waited, holding her stance. No one came to help her, but their eyes met hers and the faces turned up in disgust and horror and the sickness that stood on that day in summer's full heat.

She breathed heavy and spoke strongly, "Water! Can I just get a glass of water?!"

The owner whispered to a young Latina girl as Wormwood walked away and sat at an empty table. The air was silent but full of grease. As the young Latina stumbled to her table with a plastic glass full of iced water, she did not look Wormwood in the eye and almost ran away.

Wormwood stared at the glass as the gothic ghost of an apparition spoke, "It is filled with piss and pubic hairs."

But it was too late as she started to drink it and spit it on the floor as he was right. She jerked it away from her mouth and looked at the yellow liquor rimmed with fuzz. She gagged and stood up, reached into her shirt, and slammed a twenty dollar bill on the table but threw the toxic glass unto the floor and violently stormed back to her car without a word.

The nameless ghost spoke as they marched, "Where is the why in how you paid them?"

She mumbled out loud, "They have less than me and the nothing of the righteous ever goes away."

As she opened the car door with her crying eyes and a sweat covered arm, the angels started to cry again, "It was written in blood before it was written in stone. The prophecy has been fulfilled."

She looked to the west sky with one foot in the car, circling men growled like translucent things with wings above the massively crowded sidewalk. She got in and locked the car door, but as she went to turn it on, the old Honda's battery was dead as dirt. She tried it a couple more times, however, she realized that the machine they put on her car must have killed the damn battery. The tears in her eyes became heavier now, and she thought to call 911 and began frantically looking for her thirty-dollar burner phone under every crevice and even in her bag but yielded nothing. The visions of her family's murder creeping in her mind, her face began to sweat and cry at the same time as she sat in her car in the burning heat of summer somewhere in the ghetto of Los Angeles.

Chapter 19

In Between Mirrors

The voices of a thousand angels break through the bright blue sky, "It was written in blood before it was written in stone. A prophecy has been fulfilled."

For whom is the "I"

Water comes like a light in the sky

To whom are you oh me! Oh my!

Dismal days in this hot summer sun

To grandeur, to glory, you
are the chosen one

Be awaken in your trap

Your face can give people a heart attack

With the hands of the devil and
the mind of the sacrificial lamb

The court calls you to your name in truth

The way you walk can't give a damn

To the highest, to glory that is uncouth

Bleed the blood of the chosen one

We know exactly who you are

Without your mind, you won't go far

Your name! Your name is
burned on our arms

If you heard it, you'd be in alarm

For thy kingdom, thy power, thy glory

Eternal righteous will let your
cup always be fulfilled

The burden you bear in the
marks on your skin

God knows you will have
to play death to win

"For ye is a profound prophylactic pro-
phetic of God with the light of the morning
star that comes at the end of time," a heav-
enly voice shot down to Wormwood where
she sat festering in her blood.

She looked forward as the shadowy
presence that was behind her spoke, "I am
only for you, and you are only for me."

Her mind was wasted with tongues and
torture; she spoke in wild whispers, "For if
you are the devil and I am a joke, we came
through time in the cards. I am a nameless
joker who kills her twin and then pin the
Jack of Hearts, making a pair, who burned
the instruction card and took the universe by
breaking the pad out of the box with a hop."

He whispered, "I love you. This world is a dream that's made for you."

She smiled through the tears, "Pimm's Cup champions! I won you in this game."

Chapter 20

Psychotic Breakfast with a Side of Insanity

She heard a knock on her window, it was an older Mexican man with a mustache. His back was to her, his clothes dirty with paint like he had just been on a construction job.

He waved with a smile, "Can I buy you some lunch? There's a restaurant on the other side of the street."

Wormwood didn't trust that he was not with the cult.

She frowned as she rolled down the window, "Sorry. I am not for sale! I am not a prostitute!"

The older man's brown eyes shined, "I know, I know. I just want to talk to you."

She looked to the ghost and he said, "Go clean up in their restroom but know that you are mine alone."

Arising from the car, the street was filled with people as the tribesmen were still chanting but the rest looked like normal high school kids walking and taking pictures with their phone.

"Stand tall and show no mercy," the shadow man whispered in her ear.

She stood and walked as the musta-chioed stranger waved. All six foot of her was having tough time walking through the parking lot past the bushes. Dizzy with woe to meet him.

She met him without a word as they crossed the busy street silently, and she could tell that there was something off. He knew something she didn't.

The small Greek restaurant was empty, but as soon as Wormwood walked in the door, the owner started to scream at them to leave. The owner wouldn't shut up until the older Mexican man reassured her over and over again that they were here together just to get some food, and then they would leave.

Feeling unwelcomed and filthy, while they were waiting, Wormwood ran straight off to the bathroom. Slamming the door and rushing to get toilet paper to wash her blood legs and privates off. The blood was already down to her knees and had stained more than half of her pants. Hearing them still arguing, she washed her hands and left the bathroom.

The owner, an old woman with a mean looking wrinkled face stared her down something fierce. She looked at the menu, but all she wanted was water. The man ordered her a cheeseburger, but when she reached into her boot and tried to pay with a twenty-dollar bill, but he wouldn't let her. Finally, the lady just took her money out of her hand and gave her back $10.50. She didn't want him to pay, and she sure as hell didn't want a cheeseburger or, for that matter, any food at all. In his slimy, pushy way and how he would not let anyone say no to him, made Wormwood want to ditch him and fast. She put the $10.50 on the table by the corner and sat down.

She saw the ghost that was following her sitting next to her, and he spoke in a delicate but strong voice, "Let's get the hell out of here!"

She was getting up as the mustachioed stranger came up beside her and put the sad faint cheeseburgers down. He sat quickly and noticed her money on the table and tried to snatch it right up but she slammed her hand down first. Then he tried to lift up her hand and get the money, and he was smiling in the oddest way a person could look. She pushed the money into her boot and started to storm out the door.

Just then he yelled, smiling from ear to ear, "Do you know what those men were doing to you in the car last night?" as he laughed.

She spun around and said the first thing that came to mind, "Well, in America, you are allowed to practice any religion!" Then she walked to the door and back up and across the street.

She was at the crosswalk when she noticed a short Armenian man with many gold chains around his neck and a cell phone in his hand waving at her with both arms. He ran to meet her and just started screaming, "The car has been here for too long! You can't live in your car. You can't live in your car! You need to leave right now! Right now!"

"My car's battery is dead. I can't move it." Wormwood began to ask him to use his phone to call the cops, but he cut her off.

He yelled, "What are you? Fucked in the head! Get out of here!"

With no choice, Wormwood turned and began walking down the street past the Greek restaurant, away from the whole scene.

Marching on, crossing the streets in full sweat, blood, and tears, she had an ominous feeling that she was being followed.

Chapter 21

Calamity Insanity

A broom away from the Black Mass
and I am straight for salvation

A hex and a tragic trauma-filled night as
I live my nightmare; wayward soldiers
would know the blind leading her shadow

In the hottest broken city sun,
sweat dripping from my skin

A march for memories past the thirst, dry
our throat in highness hangman's grasp

Black souls chase the pestilence fool
but it's the fool who makes the rules

A whim and a prayer away from
madness, minds reality clasp

Crimsoned sky, swirling wings laying on
the hope of fool of loves lost tragedy

Wanting, racing, screaming, crying, crazy
but marching on sorrowful led from the east

And then the voice started screaming loud
enough to make the hair rise on the back of
her neck.

"I am Tucroc, and we're here to rape and murder you because of who you are," the voice screamed.

With a scream and a whisper, she rebuked the devil who was the beast, and the wayward soldier marched on to the death. The sun was low and cracked as she sat down next to a tree in an alcove to take to the blood of the past and gazed upon a tree and spied Pey watching her from a computer. And with the aging haze of the violet light etching the night, the tree grew but died into Dante's *Inferno*. Then she saw the souls of her rapists weaving into the tree, and the seven heads of men who were made to represent the seven goats of the Apocalypse were cast into the Inferno.

As she lay with the ghost of the gothic man around her, she asked him his name.

Carved out of stone, the Casper whispers, his periwinkle eyes gazing to the dusk; the seven men cast in stone tree glazed in the moonlight's shadow, the world beckons the night black as Pey sat and stared from a military computer.

Souls turn inside out

Bleed the blood of stone

Weave in dust

Repeat all stigmata mellow hell

Time set slow motion

She spoke aloud, "So who is this hollow of a man who follows me to my grave?"

Gabriel spoke, "He is Balthazar Razadul himself, and he is your angel."

She gaped at the gothic hologram. "Well I want to be with my cherub angel Balthazar Razadul and kiss him."

"To be with your angel in our life will be one of constant sorrow," Gabriel said.

"Do you swear to live a life with your invisible husband at your side? It was you alone who are betrothed to me," Balthazar Razadul whispered in her ear.

"Till forever after always, I love you." Wormwood teared up again.

Chapter 22

Symphony of Love
in a Hard Place

Clair de Lunatic and Balthazar Razadul read in the tune of Clair de Lune:

As Balthazar Razadul comes to me in my darkest hour and as Balthazar Razadul's eyes reflect the moons as we doth lay in the Inferno, I am what death is and have become this sacrifice and a Clair de Lunatic. Oh, what I have become. I can only gaze at you and fall in love.

And as the angel hovers and weeps, I have but one secret left to keep. That I want monogamy with thy as I lead us into this eternity; as the first Rider of the Apocalypse, I want you in between my space and my hips.

Well pestilence, I am yours and yours alone as I hold you and drive you to the phone where you can commit yourself to me, but after what Anubis has in store for thee, I will be followed to a safe home and never leave you alone.

They held each other through the night, she'd whispered sweet things in the misty gray etchings from the Inferno when the sun peeked then arose.

Terror and Naranjas

The day was already hot, and the screams of Tucroc started again that he was going to rape and gangbang Wormwood, but she didn't let that snap her stride. Archangel Michael appeared and told her how he was trying to condemn Peter Florin—willed that woe he was alive. Let him be condemned to the depths of the Inferno.

He led them to a tree where she sat and rested. She was blind to some visions that a choir of high angels sat in order like Saint Thomas Aquinas built heaven; she cleared her thoughts and tried to ignore the screams of Tucroc preaching how they were going to rape and gangbang her. She boldly spoke, "I wish to be held in hand with Balthazar Razadul, the sixth son of God for he is whom I love, and I wish to hold to my baptism and be Catholic." Screams and gasps all around

as she continued to speak to them through
the tree.

I am Catholic

As I writhe through this
hemorrhaging headache

Is that which the Black Mass of
Balthazar Razadul, you walk in my
wake holding me in shame

As you let the martyr go blind

Of the unholy to the unhappy

Hosanna was pulled from
the sky into the plain

We rot

They burn

He freezes

Only to yearn of a death set to
water that bears no light

I am Catholic

Lucifer is the morning star

We own the blood that is
heavens in contempt

Those crying eyes can hide in the wild

For I am the oldest child

The first, the last, the Lord itself

Preach the choir and hold yourself

We rot

They burn

He freezes

We kneel

Rebuke our given name to a
man who lived before.

Now screams let out as she gazed away
and saw an image of a gutted dog beside her.
It was time to move on.

As dusk was falling, still rambling on,
Balthazar Razadul and Wormwood marched
under the highway overpass that was a tunnel
while pink magic arrow visions rushed past
her and led her on a path. With a charming
voice from the sky, souls who were attached

to a mortal body somewhere in New York, he sang into the wind and almost cried, "Look into my eye. I am going to say goodbye. Hell yes!" Lazarus screams.

But Gabriel spoke harshly, "David Bowie never knows where General Sherman is going!"

Then again, he sang, "They know God exists because the devil told them so."

Balthazar Razadul spoke, "David Bowie, we are walking through the life of Job to stand at the wheel of time that Ezekiel prophesied about so Wormwood could reign eternally in new Valhalla in front of Anubis on the streets of Boyle Heights."

Lazarus said, "Well I'm gunna call the cops on you, where are you now?"

A year ago, in a cool little town next to Vail called Minturn, she wrote a version of Macbeth on Facebook with famous people, and it confessed to Oedipus, but then she deleted it. But it caught the attention of the famous people, and David Bowie found her in a dive bar. He walked to her and said, "Don't you know who I am?" Then he looked upon her right hand that had a star shape made of her veins and her hair that was part electric blue with white, blond hair on the top and he started kissing her neck.

But when Adam and his little junkie buddy saw that David Bowie was kissing her neck, he jumped him and tried to beat him up until David Bowie ran away.

I got drama that couldn't be stolen.

You and me in a boat of sadness filled with
the tears of Lucifer's kingdom come.

"You scream my name aloud.
Damn it to the world below!"

David Bowie cried like a baby.

"To the watchtowers in the center of things
facing east will be Yesod, and you will
stand in the kingdom when it comes,"

Lucifer bellowed.

Psycho prophecy be not a broken for
the tears that couldn't be spoken.

In the path you took where no rules
made, this was always coming.

Wreathed in the depths of sadness,
constantly in the stream of madness,
you should know your name.

Chapter 23

Memories and First Glances

Still cringing, crying, and shaking from the blood and sweat, she ran into the convenience store at the back end of the intersection that seemed to dip into nowhere. Her voice cracked as she asked the older Korean man for a glass of water. She was sobbing, but he kicked her out at the frightening sight of the six-foot heavily tattooed bleeding, crying crazy girl with sun-bleached, matted hair and General Sherman's piercing eyes. Outside, she quickly hid behind a car, curled on the ground, not wanting to be seen, but the car started to move. "Quickly, come and see!" Balthazar Razadul ghostly hand reached out to hers as she got up with a wiggle and shake.

At the front of the intersection, she turned the corner, a planet vision came over her and shone down from heaven. A vision of heaven with three moons in trine and three suns in trine set on top of the garden of enlightenment balance on the plain in Messeroth. It was the highest kingdom of heaven, and only the chosen dead dwelled upon it with the rebirth of the earth. It had colors that no human eyes had seen before. She stared at it, held it in her hand, and then the incident was gone. She looked up and saw this strange man who was standing on the balcony, not in Yesod but on the kingdom, in the flesh with a camera crew—he was filming her. He screamed in a way as of not to be human, "Truth is beauty, beauty is truth."

She gritted her teeth—wreaked in her own blood—and, through the tears, asked, "What are you barking about? Truth is only in the telling as familiar as the third Rider of the Apocalypse, famine." This man who had killed her family and dedicated it to Balthazar Razadul and burned Balthazar Razadul's name in family's mansion lawn. The coming of the children of Cain. The why of it all and tragedy that it meant.

The perfect man—dressed in all black, a boa of feathers around his neck with goth Doc Martens—said, "Your cult has ushered in the children of Cain. They call me the Mephistopheles of Los Angeles."

The demon that was Cain flashed in front of her eyes, embedding his seal across the sky.

As she sighed, the world went into slow motion; with the pull of the busy intersection, Mephistopheles explained his religion in a slow powerful way.

"You have been invited to eat the young.
Be a witch, be a witch, be a witch.

"Bind with my blood. Take a knife.
Cut yourself thrice. Mate with me.
I will rape you and dirty your blood
with mine together with others who
are in my nest for all my sorcery.

"One better than Balthazar Razadul.

"Cast in reverse in Revelation.

"I will get you pregnant as you're an estrus and eat your child and live forever.

"Dance on the fire in the plain moonlight and curse the Son.

"Be a witch, be a witch, be a witch."

Wormwood sat down, looked up at the stars in the sky, and said to a vision of Gabriel, "I am not a woman. I have a small star marker dick inside my pointed vagina called a penis. They made a star that could walk on water, and this is me. For no son of men could ever walk on water. Hermaphrodite is me. No slave will I be, and no witch but on prophecy will I be."

She sat on the bus station bench, and without a wink of the eye, the shadow man called Balthazar Razadul pulled out his sword. She looked at him and knew he was marking her for himself.

The watchtower appeared and the riddlers of Anubis, the god of death in Egyptian lore, and in the Freemason's bible, he is called the greeter.

On the wall that was made of brick, John of Revelation's eyes were cast in shadow, and eyes were cast out. Across the street, Pey was chained to the 7/11 drink station, and there were two jackasses, one a dead ghost and the other his living best friend joking together and staring at her through the silence.

There was a light in the sky, and music started playing in the background. It was "Ave Maria." A spotlight from the hill at the back of the intersection arose on an Egyptian Colosseum in blue light, then cast in sand color. An alien god with a large cone head walked in quickly wearing holy Egyptian robes.

When he turned to face her, she flashed the "W" sign of Horus and immediately turned it upside down so he would know what she was.

Anubis began, "So it is I who hits you at the center of this Mayan Armageddon. I mean to end this world like I did Machu Picchu with a fire-eating snake from the sky. It is I, Anubis!" This was said in a bold unfounded voice for a time before when there were gods upon this earth from another age.

Just then, a group of Mexicans opened the door to their car and whistled at her as if she was working the streets for money. She stared viciously at them with a rage and a passion of a fire of a thousand suns that could not walk on water. They slammed the door shut and sped off in fright with tires burning.

"I am no whore!" she screamed with her whole body shaking.

"They murdered my family and my pugs. They chased me out here and electrocuted me in a Black Mass. I am a homeless madman righteous on prophecy."

Anubis turned and held out his huge hand in this age of Aquarius, "I am Armageddon. You, Wormwood, are supposed to be the golden one when God walks this earth, but they treat you like a mouse in a trap. And it is you who remains nameless, you shapeless thing. I can only see you being bred in Yesod."

Chapter 24

The Wheel of Time

Cursed not to love John of
Revelation and the wrath of the

Son growing shadow in my womb

Bare the blood, dose the same

Creating game, growing in seven shadows

Blind the sun, starvation to the dog star

Death to the one who waits

Dancing on his shallow grave

Singing Psalms for your
backward ego trip from hell

We will dare to wake in your
shadow behind your dream

Oh! John of Revelation. Hangman hang
tough. It's a shame to condemn the man
who bears the blood he does the same

He will have no child with me

No sixth son should smile on my eyes

No time will walk on water but me

I am no son of man, and no child I will bare

But the sun in the sky I do declare is in my
humble blood; I will not be bred for I am
the *last* in this line who draped in madness.

Anubis walked to the back of the holographic
Egyptian Colosseum and began to turn a lever
on an old machine that looked like it was for
seeing through time and space. His eyes were
mad as they met hers. An owl started to rise
on a stick, ascending upward as he moved the
throttle. The magnitude of a car moving in
slow motion could not see the grandeur of
the event that was going on. Mephistopheles,
still standing high above the balcony across
the street in the flesh with a camera crew and
the rest of the world diseased, was hypnotized

by the sound of the universe buzzing around in slow motion.

Wormwood, shaking and crying, was covered in her period blood, her hair ratted up and bleached by the sun. She stood looking to Balthazar Razadul and remembered something the stork said to the owl: as in life as in death, there is no constant time as love but only in the war that mankind creates within themselves.

Wormwood screamed, "I will cut out my left eye from where Lucifer has possessed me all my life and then cut off my left arm where I have this very meeting tattooed on my elbow at this wheel of time before you hold any power over me!

"To these scums and the seed of men who have bled upon the earth for their own spoils and toils of war, let the power be to strike them down with the comments so profound it breaks the ground and passes the earth from the sun. Let them call it Wormwood and know the girl that I am, who the angels call the Lord, wants to look everyone straight in the eye and say you will kill yourself when the sun dies, and that's how you will meet God in the sky." She folded her arms and looked at Balthazar Razadul.

"To hell with them. Call it the rapture," Balthazar Razadul seemed to smile.

Gabriel spoke, "Cover your eyes now, child."

Wormwood covered her eyes with her filthy hands.

Gabriel spoke, "But at the start of the daybreak, time sped up. Anubis hung himself."

Chapter 25

When the Sun Died

Never in vain.
Counts like iron in threes, then
drop the noose from the treetops.
When the sun beats blood,

The hangman's pale hands turn to the four
horsemen to come just as the prophecy is
being forgiven when the sun is cursed.

And comes the gravedigger who
will have its fun for not in dirt

but in the air, and the bodies will
land everywhere on every tree

only to promise to bend a knee
before the Son of God

In the sky to ascend to heaven
in the kingdom most high.

While the water runs bitter, the
human race will cease to be.

Oh! But one thousand years after
me and the last age of Aquarius

will know his name of the
Wormwood on the cross

who should have not died in vain.

The morning light whined on, and Mephistopheles and the cult who were following her began to speak again, "Mephistopheles will rape you. Go to his bed." Over and over that was all they said.

She tore her attention away from the dissolving Colosseum and, still crying and shaking, looked upon the cracked cement lights from the sky that appeared in circles with fairylike-looking witches pointed in the direction from where she just came, the opposite side of the street. There were beautiful pastel portraits of a dark woman with a wand pointing down to the apartment building; she began following as the cult wildly chanted loudly.

She opened the door to the building and knocked furiously on the first door. A Korean family looked out slowly and then slammed the door in her face. She cried, "I just want a shower and someone to call the cops."

The cult screamed after her, "Go in that room and you will be raped by Mephistopheles."

They chanted it over and over. She thought she was done for and sat down weeping. Invisible, Balthazar Razadul came to her softly and spoke, "Turn right, false light you see on the ground is the path to judgement to the west."

Chapter 26

Dawn Begins with
a Taste of Mace

Her rambling mind was in tears; she got back and marched to the street where she saw a Mexican woman with a cart of juices across the street where the Colosseum once glowed like blue glass. She swallowed hard, then grabbed two dollars from her boots but, in shock, could not speak aloud. As she approached, the lady did not stand back but always smiled, took her money, and gave her two small glasses of mango juice. Wormwood managed a thank you. Though she was weeping and the ongoing headache felt like death was upon her brain, probably caused by whatever the hell of a machine they put on her car, she could barely speak a word but only in her mind to invisible Balthazar Razadul. The world spun as the taste of the fresh cold juice hit her lips. The sun was rising, but she noticed now that people in the cars were screaming at the sight of her with her hair covered in blood, ripped in madness, bleached by the sun, curled dreadlocks.

She looked to the sky and whispered, "Oh, am I an absolute abomination?"

"Oh ye prophet of God who comes with the light of the morning star, you have been cast to a dreary, horrifying, abused life, and they are going to burn you alive! Save your skin for it is the Savior whom you worship," said the angel of the Lord as the angel left her.

She trashed the plastic glasses and began again to march east to look for a police car or a pay phone, but she had only fifty cents in her boots.

Walk the line on faith alone

Then the cult began to chant

Heroin youth, heroin youth, heroin youth

Your love of the rush will be your living end

We killed your family to end your fate

Heroin youth, heroin youth, heroin youth

Your love of bloodlust, death will
be your end for we killed the Id

The end and the all becoming
and blamed it in your name

Heroin youth, heroin youth, heroin youth

You have no one, and nothing is
all that meets this bitter end.

Over and over for a mile down the
street, she marched in black sheer madness.
She looked down the cross street to see an
abandoned mattress where she wanted to lay
down, but Balthazar Razadul pushed her on.

"Do not retreat. They are all around you,"
the invisible Balthazar Razadul whispered.

People began to honk at her, screaming in Spanish that she was "a nasty thing" from their cars. In full tears, she marched on; and three blocks later, she saw it: a monument with flowers all around it and a stake where she was to be burned alive. Pey was there ready to light the fire. On the other side of the street was a pay phone next to a small wood picnic table in front of a Mexican storefront where a man was just opening it up.

Blood dripped down as she found her fifty cents and called 911, recited the address on the pay phone, and managed to speak.

"They killed my family. I am out of control of reality. I have nowhere to go. Will you please commit me? I have insurance. Please, please, please pick me up."

"An officer will be with you shortly," said 911 operator.

She began to cry again and sat down at the picnic table. The nice Mexican man, who was opening the store, overheard her conversation on the pay phone and gave her blue Gatorade but stared at her with sullen concern.

If the police were disinterested and didn't come in time, she avoided looking at the monument of which she would surely be burned instead she stared at the wood of the picnic table, but it changed right in front of her to dragons holding one another.

Voices sang from the stars, familiar voices; by the tree where she was to be tied to burn her alive, she saw bushes of wood to start the fire hidden behind on a small plot of land that was encased in chain-link fences. And there, out of the corner of her eye, was the man she was calling Pey (whose real name was Kip Malone).

Chapter 27

Silence on Wheels

Eyes were looking to the sky

Burn, burn, burn

Twist and turn, turn, turn

See how they yearn for the ashes in the skies

To hypnotize the heretics' eyes with surprise

As the devil lies and gruesome guys

Balthazar Razadul despise so forgo the wise

For crying ways of ashes and lashes

Of Lucifer's due the damnation will come

But only to you, Pey

There may come a day in the month of May

That the smoke will rise only known by thy

For those who drink the fresh
water from the pitcher

Will turn the stars ever quicker

To a doomsday as bitter as
the divine Norse time

And things as sweet as honey will never
be funny to those who bear the line

Burn, burn, burn

Escape through the skies and never
bare a child to ride a red horse
in the Mormon prophesy

A three whole seconds later, the cop car pulled
up on the busy street. She ran to the car, her
bloodstained pants leaving quite a mark on
the wooden picnic table.

"Are you the girl who called us?" asked a
young blond officer.

Wormwood could barely speak, quickly going right past him and trying to open the cop car looking for safety.

Balthazar Razadul spoke with her, guiding her words (even though no one could hear him but her), "I am not in the right state of mind." She could barely get the words out because that machine that electrocuted her car gave her a splitting migraine, and her voice was harsh from screaming.

The caring officer grabbed the door open. He didn't seem to mind her current look or her bleeding madness.

"Let's get you off the street. We know where to take you."

She slid into the back seat. The officer passed though the partition hole an interesting looking water bottle. She ripped it open and poured it into her dry mouth. They drove away and started to ask her some questions, but then the smell hit. And they all went silent. It was the smell of blood, period blood, dirt, and death—all rolled into a stench from hell. Silence.

Wormwood closed her weeping eyes but saw a vision of Balthazar Razadul in the hanged man position, falling down an ancient wall, spinning on the end of a rope down the vertical path.

"Dragged to the depths of the seas for my path goes on forever with thee," Balthazar Razadul said to Wormwood. Wormwood's head was spinning, she could not speak and had a pounding headache. The cops were silent. The smell was strong, and the vibe was cryptic.

The police pulled up to a medical building in the center of the city. Without a word, they led her out of the car to the door. The waiting room was packed with a bunch of pedestrians, but she didn't have to do anything to make her presence known as a nurse gasped, ran to her side, and pulled her away from the cops who said nothing more.

Clean and Bound

Weeping, Wormwood followed the nurse to the back of the psych ward right through the lobby. Wormwood sat down and saw a vision of her pug gutted in the front yard of her grandmother's old mansion.

"They killed them all," she screamed wildly, shaking and staring at the nurse who took her things away from her: her grandfather's wallet with his name engraved on it, the book of the *Tao Te Ching*, and her dirty, stained Ugg boots.

As the nurse went to go lock them away, Wormwood had a vision of the Riders of the Apocalypse. She was in a psychotic delirium as she envisioned herself as death from above, riding a white horse. Laughter broke out among the angels as Balthazar Razadul

screamed with delight, "At least you're safe
now."

The hangman's wish

As the flames lick the sky, as I
know no mercy say I, the shadow
for death's cruel design

Made of fire and ash, it would give the
stars back, but the sun will surely die

Cry away the action and pain

Tie a noose, don't make it loose, and
hang yourselves with God's grace;
you will know your shame

The world will go on just fine with
one third of the earth dead in time

Say, the hangman be I

So dance upon the air and
meet God in the sky

"It's the rapture," says I

Then the nurse came and said, "Let's get you into the shower." The dimly lit handicap accessible hospital shower was a welcomed sign. She ripped off her cruel sun-bleached yoga pants, which had pooled a sea of blood and dark tissue, that quickly hit the floor in a seething wave onto the stagnant pristine white floor. She threw the sweaty, dirt-encrusted navy-starred tank top at the nurse who gasped again.

"I just take these to the trash then," the nurse spoke in a harsh whisper as she closed the door.

Then she jumped into the cool freezing water. She stood facing the showerhead letting the water hit her face, hard and cold, as it soaked her now dreadlocks of sun-drenched auburn mane. And she thought to Balthazar Razadul as the blood hit the ground in horrible, scarlet-red chunks:

Ring around the roses, a
pocket full for Moses

Ashes, ashes, we wash away the sin

So we can begin again

Baptize by blasphemy and encrusted by
the sun as we sing in the midnight

Oh, speak unto me, God's mighty children

Whisper in the abyss, sing in the wave
and whimsy, come hither ever after

Ring around the one as our mind holds tight

Dust to dust, in Wormwood we trust

As the flood is after the two of us

Knowing that we must save the ones who
fight for the fairness of God's true believers

Catch a cold, have a fevered
dream of hell's nightmare

Let the water wash away all the sin
we lived through yesterday

"Balthazar Razadul! Oh, my righteous
love! How does this lunatic deserve you?"
Wormwood smiled at the shadowy figure

and danced in the shower as she lost herself in the joy of the water.

"Clean yourself off, dust yourself off, and deliver yourself to Balthazar Razadul himself," Balthazar Razadul and about a dozen angels chanted all at once.

With that, the nurse came in with hospital scrubs for her and took her to a large room with many beds. They went to an empty bed, and the nurse laid her down and gave her a blanket.

Blood on a Straitjacket

Wormwood closed her wet, tired eyes, and Balthazar Razadul made a crippling sound right under her in the small hospital bed.

All of sudden, she heard the great ticking of a clock; and as she opened her eyes, it seemed to her that all the madmen in the large room full of beds seemed to be moving in slow motion to the beat of the clock. Not only that, but their bodies also seemed to be made of sand and blue light.

The cryptic ballet of the madmen's motion shocked her vision. The world seemingly changed into a vision of bizarre-shaped writing. She could feel Balthazar Razadul's arms around her, the clock counting one and on and on. The mesmerizing mental patients outlined in blue did not look at her knowing the world was or seemed to be hypnotized.

Chapter 28

Baptized Bastard

Don't pray for me because my
ego thinks I can hear you

My specialties include religious fan
fiction and surprise Haldol injections

My life in a straitjacket is like
the music in the Bible

With all the melodies ravished in blasphemy

Living a life with no regret begets
to a future of only lamenting

Hesitating before you smile

And never being able to communicate
the unspeakable things

You have seen

Rejecting any type of therapy but the
comfort of a confession booth

Shots to keep you sane

Shots to keep you safe

Shots to control your reality

Day to day woes include

Brushing your hair and ignoring the
cryptic voices that speak in tongues
that only you can understand

Outside, I am a picturesque Leviathan
of white privileged youth

Inside, I am just wondering when
the demons will come to call

So I can scream like the
baptized bastard I am

The mirror reflection, what was once sacred
is now a living rapture of self-loathing

Oh! How many colors can you paint of crazy

Before you paint it black with denial

"Get sedated," Balthazar Razadul
whispered in her ear.

With a shock of electricity, Wormwood jumped from her bed and started running around the psych ward, loudly screaming as she ran past the nurse's station and through an open door that led to a security center. The look on the man's face was priceless as she spun around back to her bed. But two steps back and she was being tackled by a male orderly, and three nurses came to her on the floor with a syringe and a straitjacket. One of the nurses cried, "This is a lethal dose!"

As they continued to force her into the straitjacket, they carried her into the isolation room. She was dazed with a massive headache, but she could feel the blood of her period ran over the straps of the horrifying straitjacket.

Laying on the bed, she began to see the walls change as she fell under sedation, unfolding like a treasure map that ended with the face of Mephistopheles turning into a dragon. Seconds later, the drug took hold of her, and she fell dead asleep.

Interlude

Wormwood awoke to a beam of light and a feel of motion. An EMT who was a woman with dark hair sat above her, smiled, and said, "We're taking you to a safe place."

In a blink of an eye, she fell fast asleep again as the golden light shone down upon her from the small ambulance window.

A male orderly picked her up when she stopped shaking and put her back in bed. She stayed unconscious for a number of hours that seemed like years in slow motion.

She awoke in the dead of night and was not able to walk, move, or talk. She could only think to the angels and Balthazar Razadul, but they were screaming when she woke up.

"You will not see heaven. You will not see hell. You will not see anything but Valhalla," the angels cried and repeated it over and over again.

"I am the nutty Nietzsche who you did not see coming!" Her brain was still pounding.

And with that, she fell asleep until Monday where she awoke to a social worker. A small brown-eyed lady who looked shocked when Wormwood said hello, although her face seemed to be frozen from the seizure.

"Hello. Nice to see you up. My name is Maria, and I have been working on your file. The other hospital found your insurance card and sent you here. Do you have any idea why you are here?" She smiled but looked cautiously at Wormwood.

Wormwood tried to speak but her voice was small and rough, and she could barely move her mouth. "I-I had visions of a cult killing my family," she stammered but could barely get the words out. She started to cry.

"Oh my, that's horrible. Let me try calling their cell phone. If you sign some paperwork and give me permission, I can see what's going on." She whipped out a piece of paper from her notebook, and Wormwood tried to make her hand move. With that, the social worker headed back to the nurses' station.

Then Wormwood heard a familiar voice from the sky. It was Ebe. It was kind but assertive like that of an older Jewish man who was wise and had a good sense of humor. "For what do you see in tomorrow's awakening? Or are ye not a prophet of God's true will?" said Ebe in a clear voice spoken from above.

I remember last summer, thought Worthless Wormwood, *when I had just bro-*

ken up with Adam again when we lived in San Pedro. It was hotter than all hell outside.

"I remember that red box of a shithole we lived in," Balthazar Razadul cried.

"Don't tell a lie to Ebe. What drugs did you absolutely OD on?" Archangels yelled in her ear.

I was coming down off meth, but it was the first and only time I ever did it. And it is a disgusting drug, she thought.

"So it is God's will that you just sit and almost kill yourself on drugs?" Ebe asked with sensitive ease.

"I left the house with Balthazar Razadul and Archangel Gabriel and Lucifer and a small group of angels who I was always with," Wormwood tried to remember.

"It's not a bad thing, sitting around and talking to angels all day, especially if you're on marijuana," Gabriel smiled.

"I tried to check into a cheap hotel to be away from Adam, but it happened in there, the underground parking lot." Wormwood cried. "I saw a very long vision about the creation of heaven, and then a longer vision of the horrible future of this world." Wormwood said.

"What does the future hold?" Ebe asked.

"Nuclear winter holocaust," Wormwood said grudgingly.

"Oh my!" yelled Ebe.

"Nuclear war with China. It's hard to remember, but I think they hit Las Vegas first. Then a comet knocks the earth out of rotation, so it's a constantly dark winter. And the remaining people kill themselves," she said with gloom and depredation.

"The rapture," Balthazar Razadul said.

"Dear God," said Ebe.

All of a sudden, a nurse came in. Her name was Miriah and told me the good news about my parents who were still alive.

Chapter 29

Grand Mal Seizure

The night was heavy and dark when Wormwood awoke from her sedation. There was no one else in the stark ward but a light in the door frame and a noise from the crowded nurses' station.

Without thinking, she got up and walked to the door. Her headache was enormous, and she could feel pulsating blood around her brain. She walked to the hallway, and as soon as she hit the light and looked right to the nurses' station, it happened.

Snap, crackle, and pop. Electric hop fried her spine. Wormwood was convulsing on the ground. Eyes blinding. Hands shaking. Back frying. It was a grand mal seizure and hurt like she could feel the last beat of her heart sound and wanted it to sound no more. Unspeakable pain in her brain.

With the sparkle and lick of electric bite,

Pestilence can't scream in fright

Fear is not allowed in all, but
with a flash and a moan,

I will never be alone

For what dawns on to death's back is a
snap and a click away from a heart attack

With fire on the seas of the seven
death tolls of disease, I know that I
never seem to be uncouth to thee, a
shadow of a magus, a gorgeous sight

As tears cling to his face in a day's
worst night, will a shock from a
clock in Balthazar Razadul wake

To the depths of my bowels of what's
our trouble of power, of pain in a
stranger, a maggot of a girl in danger

Checkered, checkered spots, brilliant
bursting white dots of explosion
of pain to this insane brain

As I lay in the valley of the shadow of death,
I scream with pain until there is nothing left

The next morning, she realized it had been days that she had been laying in her bed. The nurses put her in a wheelchair and took her to the front room where her parents were waiting for her. Unfortunately, they had brought Adam. They handed her a water bottle that says: Age of Aquarius.

Sad Girl be not a broken for the
tears that couldn't be spoken

In the path you took where no rules
were make, this was always coming

Grieved in the depths of sadness,
constantly in the stream of madness, it
was you who should know your name.

Chapter 30

Truth of an Honest Birth

Walks with a ghost who screams in silliness
I close my eyes when I call his name
Bound by fate, twisted hand,
and only God's blind will
As we creep to create the coming blood
Into the night dance upon the dead

Wave like necromancy sound
the pluses of their morals
It is a sin that is getting misled

Time is mirrored in the road we're on
Moon moves tight in their eyes
Smoke and ashes
Time and fascist
Niacin and lies

Wrath does not play the fool
And is not invoked by pride, it
Simply is God's will that
Suffering is the key to a road
Bathed in glory

Epilogue

Allison has led a reclusive life after she dumped Adam. She diligently takes her schizophrenic medication, but it has taken away Balthazar Razadul, which is a relief to her. At the time this was written, she believed she was talking with God, the angels, and Lucifer, the Morning Star, who had been present with her for many years. While she previously saw visions that she believed predicted the future, they turned out not to be true, and she knows she is not a prophet. However, as part of her schizophrenia disease, she often hears voices who berate, harass, and sometimes say funny things to her. She knows the voices are not real, but they sound so real to her and are very difficult to ignore. It's also challenging to function to do life's daily tasks because the voices scream at her so loudly and are triggered by so many things. The medications are working, and now that she doesn't drink alcohol or do any kind of drugs, she is much happier and more sane. However, she knows that should she go off the meds, she'll return to a very dark place. Allison is trying to live a good, simple life, writes poetry, and hopes that she'll find a soulmate.

About the Author

Allison Kanuit grew up in Southern California and had an early love for horses and cooking. She competed in the hunter/jumper division in many A-circuit shows and was the captain of her high school equestrian team. She attended the Culinary Institute of America in Hyde Park, New York, and worked in several Michelin-star restaurants in Los Angeles.

Schizophrenia has been present in her family for many generations. While she was diagnosed as bipolar and schizoaffective at about age seventeen, she thinks she suffered from early-on schizophrenia at a young age because she heard voices and was certain that people could hear her thoughts. As a young girl, she used to hear the voice of Lucifer, who was her best friend; and as the god of enlightenment and the morning star, Lucifer had a positive influence on her. As she grew older, she heard another voice, that of Balthazar Razadul, an angel who said he was Allison's boyfriend. However, that created quite a ruckus of voices from angels who constantly screamed at Allison that it was unholy to have a relationship with an angel, especially one that had escaped from the Euphrates River. Now the medications are working, and all those voices have gone away.

Allison has successfully been managing her medications, which help contain her schizophrenia, and is leading a quiet but productive life.